DOMESTIC DOGS

PUGS

by Susan H. Gray

Published in the United States of America by The Child's World®
PO Box 326 • Chanhassen, MN 55317-0326
800-599-READ • www.childsworld.com

PHOTO CREDITS
© Andre Jenny/Alamy: 17
© Associated Press: 23
© Craig Ellenwood/Alamy: 25
© iStockphoto.com/Dan Roundhill: cover, 1
© Juniors Bildarchiv/Alamy: 11, 15. 21
© Mark Compton: 27
© The Print Collector/Alamy: 9
© Purestock/Alamy: 13
© Robert McGouey / Alamy: 27
© Sieglinde Scholle: 19

ACKNOWLEDGMENTS
The Child's World®: Mary Berendes, Publishing Director;
Katherine Stevenson, Editor

Content Adviser: Pug Dog Club of America

The Design Lab: Kathleen Petelinsek, Design and Page Production

LIBRARY OF CONGRESS CATALOGING-IN-PUBLICATION DATA
Gray, Susan Heinrichs.
  Pugs / by Susan H. Gray.
    p. cm. — (Domestic dogs)
  Includes bibliographical references and index.
  ISBN 1-59296-776-0 (library bound : alk. paper)
  1. Pug—Juvenile literature. I. Title. II. Series.
  SF429.P9G73 2007
  636.76—dc22   2006022639

Table of Contents

NAME That DOG!

What dog has been around for more than 2,000 years? What dog sometimes snores when it sleeps? What dog is a favorite of kings and queens? What dog needs its face cleaned every day? Did you say the pug? You had the right answer!

5

From China to the World

No one is sure why these dogs are called "pugs." It might be because they look like a little monkey called a pug.

Pugs have been around longer than most dog **breeds**. **Emperors** in China once kept pugs as pets. That was more than 2,000 years ago. Over time, the breed spread all across the country. From China, pugs spread to Japan and Europe.

Russia

Kazakhstan

Kyrgyzstan

Mongolia

North
Korea

South
Korea

China

Yellow
Sea

Nepal

India

Bhutan

East
China
Sea

Bangladesh

Myanmar

Vietnam

Laos

South
China
Sea

The map on the left
shows where China
is on Earth. The map
on the right shows a
closer view.

7

In Europe, **royal** families raised pugs. They liked the dogs' odd faces. Pugs were also small and friendly. Kings and queens often gave them as gifts.

In 1572, a pug in Holland became a hero. He saved the life of a prince. While Prince William slept, his enemies crept up to kill him. The prince's pug started to bark. The prince woke up—just in time!

In the 1700s, a famous English painter owned pugs. His name was William Hogarth. He often put his dogs in his paintings.

Hogarth's paintings made pugs even more **popular**. More and more people wanted pugs. In time, pugs were brought to North America. Today, they are one of our most popular breeds.

Prince William is buried at a church in Holland. His grave has a statue of the prince with his pug.

William Hogarth painted this picture of himself and a pug in 1745.

9

A Lot of Dog in a Small Space

A pug's black nose and **muzzle** are sometimes called a mask.

Pugs are small, but they are well built and likable. They are only about 12 inches (30 centimeters) tall at the shoulder. They weigh about 14 to 18 pounds (6 to 8 kilograms). They have thick bodies, big chests, and strong legs.

This pug climbed to the top of a small woodpile to have a look around.

Pugs have a rounded head. Their eyes are large and dark. Their small, soft ears are folded down. Their muzzle is short, and their nose is wide. The ears, nose, and muzzle are always black. This is true even for light-colored pugs.

The skin on a pug's face is thick and loose. It forms wrinkles around the eyes and muzzle. The rest of the pug's skin is loose, too. But it is not wrinkled.

Pugs have short hair. It is light brown or black. Many pugs have a marking called a *trace*. The trace is a black line. It runs down the dog's back.

Pugs' tails are tightly curled. They do not stick up. Instead, they rest over the dog's hip.

Tan pugs are called "fawn" or "apricot."

Can you see the black trace running down this pug's back?

13

Not Known for Their Beauty

Pugs win people's hearts for many reasons. They are small and easy to care for. They are **loyal** to their owners. They are friendly and gentle with children. They get along well with other pets.

Pugs are also very smart. They can learn to be good watchdogs. They can learn when to bark. And they can learn when not to bark.

Pugs have very round eyes that stick out. Some people think this makes the dogs look funny. Others think it makes the dogs look cute!

15

Many people like pugs' wrinkled faces and big eyes. The wrinkles can make the dogs look worried or sad. Some people even put their pugs in "beauty" **contests**!

Pugs are not the quietest dogs to have around. They do not bark a lot. But their breathing is sometimes noisy! Their flat nose partly blocks their airway. So they often wheeze. They can snore loudly, too. Many people do not mind the sound. They like to hear their little dog nearby.

Snort! Snerk! This pug is breathing hard after playing in a park.

Pug Babies

Mother pugs usually have two to five puppies in a **litter**. The newborn pups are chubby and helpless. Their legs are too weak for walking. Their eyes are shut tight. They cannot hear.

They can feel things, though. They can tell when they are close to their mother. They know when their brothers and sisters are nearby. They can tell when someone picks them up.

This little pug is three days old. She has a red ribbon around her neck. This helps her owner tell her apart from the other puppies.

Even as babies, they still look like pugs. They have round heads and small ears. They have chunky bodies and thick necks. They have dark muzzles. And they have wrinkled faces.

One thing the pups do not have is a curly tail. A newborn pug's tail is straight! But soon it begins to bend upward. In a few weeks, it is nice and curly.

At first, the puppies need to stay with their mother. After five or six weeks, they start to get brave. They start to move away from their mother. Their little trips do not last long! They are not yet ready for the world. But they keep getting bigger and stronger. When they are 12 weeks old, they are ready to leave. They are ready to be with a new family.

This pug puppy is about six weeks old. It is very curious about some other dogs nearby.

21

What a Great Life!

Since long ago, people have kept pugs just as pets. These dogs were not taught to hunt. They never herded sheep or cattle. They were not trained to do any work.

Pugs owned by royalty have had very easy lives! One couple in England really treated their pugs well. The Duke and Duchess (DUTCH-ess) of Windsor owned many pugs. They took the dogs along on trips. They took someone along just to cook for the dogs.

The Duke and Dutchess of Windsor loved their pugs. Here they are in Paris in 1964.

23

Most pugs are not treated quite like that! But they do have easy lives. Some pugs have had real jobs. They have been on TV and in the movies. Some pugs have been in paintings, such as William Hogarth's.

Many pug owners **spoil** their dogs. They dress them in clothes. They buy fancy collars for them. They take them to pug get-togethers.

In some cities, owners bring their pugs to big meetings. Hundreds of people and pugs show up. The owners tell stories about their dogs. They give each other suggestions. They have pictures taken with their pets. The pugs have fun playing with each other.

Some owners buy all sorts of clothes for their pugs. They dress their dogs in skirts, T-shirts, and even pajamas!

The owner of these pugs dressed them in funny hats for a dog parade.

Caring for a Pug

Pugs need exercise to stay healthy. But sometimes they get lazy. They might lie around all day. They might eat too much. If this goes on too long, they can get heavy. Then they have trouble getting around.

Pugs' short muzzles can sometimes cause problems. The nose and skull bones are too crowded. The dogs cannot breathe easily. They make a wheezing noise. They sound as if they are not getting enough air.

Pugs are great pets for people in small homes. They do not need a big yard to play in.

This pug is playing a game of "tug" with its owner.

Sometimes when pugs run around, they start gasping for air. If this happens, they need to rest. They need to cool down. Pugs that are too heavy often have this problem.

It is easy for pugs to get too cold or too hot. They should be **protected** from hot or cold weather. Some owners have their pugs wear coats in the winter. Others hose them down in the summer.

Pugs' wrinkled faces can be a problem. The wrinkles can hold dirt. They can trap fleas and ticks. Pugs with lots of wrinkles need their faces cleaned every day. This sounds like a lot of trouble. But the owners love their dogs anyway.

Healthy pugs live to be 12 to 15 years old. Some pugs have lived to be over 20! Their owners enjoy having them around for so long.

Some pugs have problems with their knees or hips. Their bones can pop out of the joints. Animal doctors, or **veterinarians**, can fix this problem.

Pugs are happy little dogs. Sometimes they look as if they are smiling!

29

Glossary

breeds (BREEDZ) Breeds are certain types of an animal. Pugs are one breed of dog.

contests (KON-tests) Contests are meets where people or animals try to win by being the best. Some pug owners enter their dogs in beauty contests.

emperors (EM-pur-urz) Emperors are rulers of a group of countries (called an *empire*). Emperors in China owned pugs more than 2,000 years ago.

litter (LIH-tur) A litter is a group of babies born to one animal. Pugs often have four or five pups in a litter.

loyal (LOY-ul) To be loyal is to be true to something and stand up for it. Pugs are loyal to their owners.

muzzle (MUH-zul) An animal's muzzle is its nose and mouth area. Pugs have short muzzles.

popular (PAH-pyuh-lur) When something is popular, it is liked by lots of people.

protected (pruh-TEK-ted) To be protected is to be kept safe. Pugs need to be protected in hot or cold weather.

royal (ROY-ull) Royal means having to do with kings or queens. Royal families in Europe have often raised pugs.

spoil (SPOYL) To spoil people or animals is to give them whatever they want. Many pug owners spoil their dogs.

veterinarians (vet-rih-NAIR-ee-unz) Veterinarians are doctors who take care of animals. Veterinarians are often called "vets" for short.

To Find Out More

Books to Read

Hubbard, Woodleigh. *For the Love of a Pug.*
New York: G. P. Putnam's Sons, 2003.

Maggitti, Phil. *Pugs.* Hauppauge, NY:
Barron's Educational Series, 2000.

Yaccarino, Dan. *Unlovable.* New York:
Henry Holt & Co., 2004.

Places to Contact

American Kennel Club (AKC)
Headquarters
260 Madison Ave, New York, NY 10016
Telephone: 212-696-8200

On the Web

Visit our Web site for lots of links
about pugs:

http://www.childsworld.com/links

*Note to Parents, Teachers, and Librarians:
We routinely check our Web links to make
sure they're safe, active sites—so encourage
your readers to check them out!*

Index

About the Author

Susan H. Gray has a Master's degree in zoology. She has written more than 70 science and reference books for children. She loves to garden and play the piano. Susan lives in Cabot, Arkansas, with her husband Michael and many pets.